MA+HS
IS EVERYWHERE

GET IN SHAPE

Two-dimensional and three-dimensional shapes

Rob Colson

Acknowledgments and Picture credits

Published in Great Britain in 2018 by
The Watts Publishing Group

Copyright © The Watts Publishing Group,
2017

Series editor: Sarah Peutrill

Produced by Tall Tree Ltd
Design: Ben Ru occo
Consultants: Hilary Koll and Steve Mills

Every attempt has been made to
clear copyright. Should there be any
inadvertent omission please apply to the
publisher for rectification.

Dewey Classification 516.1'5

ISBN: 978 1 4451 4944 8
Printed in China

Franklin Watts
An imprint of
Hachette Children's Group
Part of The Watts Publishing Group
Carmelite House
50 Victoria Embankment
London EC4Y 0DZ

An Hachette UK Company
www.hachette.co.uk

www.franklinwatts.co.uk

Picture credits:
t-top, b-bottom, l-left, r-right, c-centre,
front cover-fc, back cover-bc
All images courtesy of Dreamstime.com,
unless indicated:
Inside front Btktan; fc, bc Pablo631; fc,
6b, Dayzeren; 1c, 14t Starserfer; 4b,
21b, 26c Mexrix; 5t Lluecke; 5c Fotyma;
5b Oocoskun; 6c Studioloco; bctr, 8tl
Offscreen; 9tr Beho206; 9b Leisuretime70;
10b Aleksandar Mirkovic; 11c Yulan; 11c
Sophy Kozlova; fccr, 11br Ffatserifade;
13tr PepeLaguarda/iStockphoto.com; fcbr,
13b Andreykuzmin; 15c Artcomedy; 15tr
Grafistart; 16r Andresr; 17br Valeriy
Kachaev; 18c 79mtk; fctc, 19b Witr;
bcc, 20bl, Dedmazay; fcbl, 20c, 30tr
Nikolais; 22c NASA; 23tr Gstudioimagen;
23b NASA; 24c, 30b Snicol24; fctc, 24b
Theblackrhino; fctr, 25tr Deomister;
25c Photozirka; 25cr Radu191289; 25bl
Thumeau; 26c Skillividden; 27t Gbuglok;

Contents

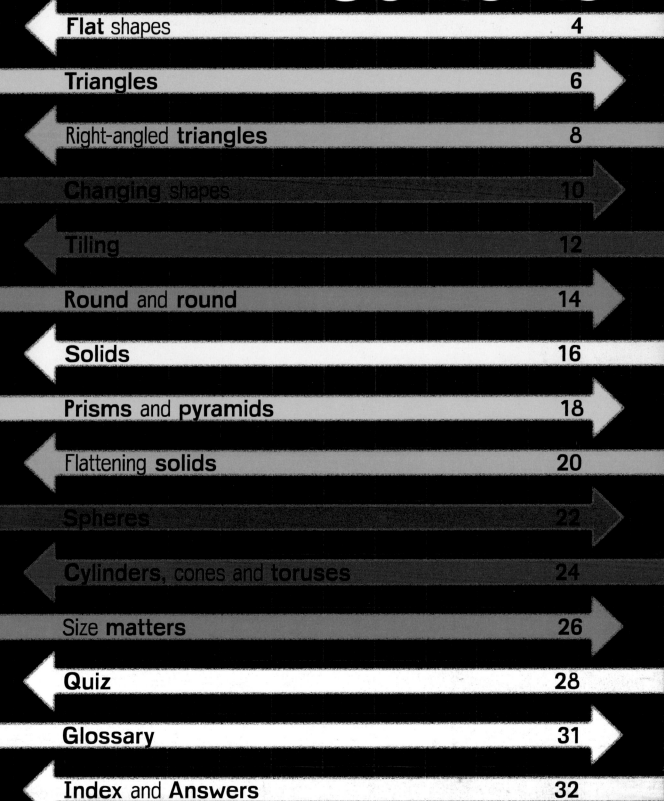

Flat shapes

We use a kind of maths called geometry to describe the shapes we see around us. We define the shapes by their properties. The simplest shapes are those with two dimensions, which we can draw on a piece of paper. They have an area but do not have a depth.

Polygons

Shapes with straight sides are called polygons. Regular polygons have sides of equal length and equal interior angles. All regular polygons can fit exactly inside a circle. Each interior angle is always less than 180°, but the more sides the shape has, the closer the angles get to 180°, and the tighter it fits inside its circle.

A **regular triangle** (also called an equilateral triangle) has **three sides** and an interior angle of **60°**

Triangle
60°

A **square** has **four sides** and an interior angle of **90°**

Square
90°

A **regular octagon** has **eight sides** and an interior angle of **135°**

Octagon
135°

A **regular octadecagon** has **18 sides** and an interior angle of **160°**

Octadecagon
160°

A regular polygon with **1 million sides** is called a **megagon**. It has interior angles of **179.9996°**. To the naked eye, it would look like a circle.

Symmetry

A shape is symmetrical if it can be flipped or turned to make the same shape.

Reflection

With reflection symmetry, one half of a shape is the reflection, or mirror image, of another. The faces of many animals show reflection symmetry – the left side is a mirror image of the right.

Rotation

If a shape can be rotated about its centre and stay the same, it has rotational symmetry. A star fish has rotational symmetry if it is rotated around an angle of 72°.

72°

Garden fence

HOUSE THIS SIDE

8 metres

6 metres

The perimeter of a shape is the total length of its sides. If you are buying fencing for a garden, you need to know the perimeter of your garden.

Sarah has a rectangular back garden that is 6 metres wide and 8 metres long. If fencing is sold in 2-metre sections, how much fencing will she need to buy for her garden?

For Sarah to solve her problem, she needs to know the perimeter of the garden minus the side that faces the house. This leaves just three sides to be fenced in. So Sarah needs

8 + 6 + 8 metres

of fencing, which is

22 m, or 11 sections.

Triangles

A three-sided polygon is called a triangle. Triangles can be described in terms of the length of their sides or the size of their angles.

What type of angle?

Equilateral triangles have equal sides and equal angles.

If you stand straight, with your legs apart, you are making an **isosceles triangle** with your legs. Isosceles triangles have **two equal sides** and **two equal angles**. They form a strong shape when you stand as an equal weight is pushed onto each leg.

An **acute triangle** is a triangle whose angles are **all less than 90°**.

A **right-angled triangle** is a triangle with **one angle at exactly 90°** (known as a right-angle).

An **obtuse triangle** has **one angle** that is **greater than 90°**.

Isosceles

75°   75°

The area of a triangle

If you multiply the **height** of a triangle by its **base**, you get the **area** of a rectangle that the triangle sits inside. The area of the triangle is equal to ½ × **the area** of this rectangle.

The equation for the area looks like this:

$$\text{Area} = hb/2$$

60°
Equilateral

<90°
Acute

90°
Right-angle

>90°
Obtuse

The adding of angles

Draw a **triangle** on a piece of paper, then cut off the **three corners** and fit them around **a single point**. The three angles fitted together will make a straight line. You can try this with any triangle and the result will be the same. This is a property of triangles – the three internal angles always **add up to 180°**.

Scalene triangles have no equal sides and no equal angles

1

2

3

1   **2**

3

All triangles have three internal angles that add up to 180°.
This comes in very useful for mathematicians.

Architects use isosceles triangles when building bridges. The shape makes the structure very strong by distributing the weight evenly.

Right-angled triangles

Right-angled triangles are triangles with one angle of 90°. They have special properties that make them hugely useful in solving many kinds of problems.

PITAGORA

Pythagoras's theorem

Around 2,500 years ago, the Greek mathematician Pythagoras discovered an amazing fact about right-angled triangles. Now known as Pythagoras's theorem, it states that:

The square of the hypotenuse is equal to the sum of the squares of the other two sides.

The hypotenuse is the side of the triangle opposite the right angle.

If you draw squares on each side of the triangle like this, the areas of the two smaller squares add up to make the area of the larger square.

c^2

c

a^2 a

b

b^2

Pythagorean triples

Pythagorean triples are special right-angled triangles that have sides with lengths that are whole numbers.

You can use a 3,4,5 right-angled triangle to check whether the corners on a carpet are right angles. Measure 30 cm along one side of the carpet, and 40 cm along the other side. If the diagonal is 50 cm long, the corner must be a right angle. If it is more than 50 cm, the corner is an obtuse angle. If it is less than 50 cm, the corner is an acute angle.

30 cm

40 cm

?? cm

a^2

+

b^2

=

c^2

To see that this is true, take four identical right-angled triangles and arrange them so that the four right-angles become the four corners of a square (you can do this with any right-angled triangle):

Now rearrange the four triangles like so:

In the first diagram, the triangles form a square with c^2. In the second diagram they form the same square with a^2 and b^2. Therefore

$$a^2 + b^2 = c^2$$

Changing shapes

A transformation is a way of changing a shape according to a set of mathematical rules.

Stretching shapes

Shapes can be distorted by transformations. A shear fixes points on one line, but shifts all other points to one side.

A stretch fixes points on one line, but moves all other points up or down.

Translation

A translation moves a shape from one place to another without changing its appearance. Each corner moves in exactly the same direction and distance.

Here, the shape of a tree has been translated exactly, but within a field of perspective lines. It is an optical illusion that tricks us into believing that the higher image is further away. Because we think it's further away, our brains tell us that it is bigger. Check for yourself with a ruler – both trees are exactly the same size!

10

Funhouse mirrors are curved in a way that shears and stretches the reflected image.

Reflection

A reflection produces a 'mirror image' of a shape. Each point on the shape is moved so that it is same distance away from the mirror line but on the opposite side.

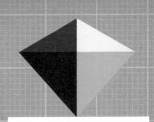

Resizing

Resizing makes a shape bigger or smaller. The change in size is described by a scale factor. For instance, a scale factor of 3 will make each side of a shape 3 times longer. A scale factor of ⅓ will make each side one-third of the length. The shapes look similar as they have the same internal angles.

Maps use really small scale factors to represent areas that may be many kilometres across. This map has a scale factor of 1:100,000, meaning that 1 km on the ground is shrunk and represented by just 1 cm on the map.

"It's on the left, right?"

"What?!!"

Tiling

Tiling, or tessellation, is the fitting together of shapes in a way that leaves no gaps between them.

Regular tessellation

Regular tessellation is tiling using just one regular shape. Only regular shapes with interior angles that divide into 360° can tessellate, as they need to be able to fit exactly around one point. This means that there are just three possibilities:

Squares
A square has angles of 90°, meaning that four squares can fit around a point.

Equilateral triangles
An equilateral triangle has angles of 60°, meaning that six equilateral triangles can fit around a point.

Regular hexagon
A regular hexagon has angles of 120°, meaning that three can fit around a point.

Regular tessellation won't work with any other shape. For instance, a pentagon (left) has internal angles of 108°. This does not divide into 360°.

Semi-regular tessellations

You can combine two different regular polygons to make tessellations. In semi-regular tessellations, the number of sides touching at each vertex (corner) are equal.

The combination above is a semi-regular tessellation of hexagons and triangles.

Islamic art

Beautiful tessellated patterns are a common feature in Islamic art. Islamic artists cover walls with self-repeating patterns that could go on forever. Can you see the reflection and rotation symmetry in this Islamic design?

Bees are experts at tiling. They construct their honeycombs using regular hexagons.

13

Round and round

A circle is a shape made from a line of points that are the same distance from another point. That point becomes the centre of the circle. We can draw a circle using a pair of compasses. One arm of the compasses stays at the centre, while the other draws the circle.

The distance from the centre to the edge of a circle is called the radius. Twice that distance gives the diameter. The distance around the outside of the circle is its circumference.

radius (r)

circumference

Pi

Once you know the radius (**r**) of a circle, you can work out its area and circumference using a special number called π or pi. Pi is the number you get when you divide a circle's circumference (**c**) by its diameter (**d**).

$$\pi = c/d \text{ or } \pi = c/2r$$

This gives the equation $c = 2\pi r$ for the circumference of a circle.
The area of a circle is equal to πr^2

Pi is a special number that goes on forever when it is written out. Here's how it starts: 3.14159265358979323846264338327950 2884197169399375105820974944592307816406286208998628 0348253421170679821480865132823066470938446095505822 3172535940812848111745028410270193852110555964462294 95493038196442881097566593344612847564823378678316527

How much pizza?

A section of a circle made by two radiuses is called a sector. A slice of pizza is a sector of the whole pizza. The angle between the radiuses determines the number of slices. This angle is equal to 360° divided by the number of slices.

Here, there are eight slices of pizza, meaning that the angle between the radiuses is 45°.

diameter (d)

45°

sector

Darts

A dartboard is a circle divided into 20 sectors. The angle between each radius is equal to 18°.

18°

Ellipses

An ellipse is an oval that looks like a squashed circle.

Unlike a circle, an ellipse does not have a centre. Instead, it has two points called its focuses. The sum of the distances from any point on the ellipse to both focuses is always the same.

$$a + b = c + d$$

Solar System
The orbits of the planets around the Sun are ellipses, with the Sun at one of the two focuses.

Focus 1   Focus 2

a   b   c   d

Solids

So far we have been dealing with shapes in two dimensions. Shapes in three dimensions are called solids.

Polyhedrons

Solids with flat faces are called polyhedrons (meaning 'many faces').

Before it is inflated, a football is an example of a polyhedron. It is made from a combination of **pentagons** and **hexagons**.

Hexagon

Pentagon

When the football is filled with air, it turns into a **sphere**. A sphere does not have flat faces, and is called a non-polyhedron solid.

Regular solids

"**Wow, I'm full of hot air**"

There are five regular solids, known as the Platonic solids, after the ancient Greek philosopher Plato, who was one of the first to describe them. Each face of a Platonic solid is the same shape and each vertex has the same angles.

Tetrahedron
four faces, each a triangle

Cube
six faces, each a square

Octahedron
eight faces, each a triangle

Dodecahedron
twelve faces, each a pentagon

Icosahedron
twenty faces, each a triangle

An impossible shape!

Mathematicians love to play around with 3D shapes and come up with 2D drawings of solids that are impossible to make. The British mathematician Roger Penrose invented the Penrose Triangle. Can you see why it would be impossible to make one?

Fair dice

If you roll a Platonic solid, each of its faces has an equal chance of landing face-up. This makes them the perfect shapes for making fair dice.

Prisms and pyramids

Parallelogram

Base

This is a pentagonal prism, with five-sided pentagons at the bases.

Prisms

A prism is a solid with two ends, or bases, that are the same shape, parallel and connected to each other by straight lines. The shape of the base gives the prism its name. The sides are parallograms – four-sided shapes with two pairs of parallel sides.

Volume of a prism
A prism's volume (V) is the area of its base (A) × its length (L): $V = A × L$

Right-prisms

A right-prism is a prism with rectangles along its sides. An allen key (left) is the shape of a right-prism with a 90° bend in it.

"This isn't my good side"

Irregular prisms

Irregular prisms have bases with irregular polygons. Houses are often the shape of an irregular right-prism, with the base on the side of the house.

Base

Pyramids

A pyramid has a flat polygon base. Each side of the pyramid is a triangle. The sides meet at a point called the apex.

A pyramid is named after the shape of its base. This is a pentagonal pyramid.

A pentagonal pyramid has:

6 faces
(including the base)
5 triangular sides
6 corners
10 edges

The number of edges on a pyramid is equal to twice the number of sides of the base. Can you see why this is?

Apex

Base

Side

Edge

Corner

Great Pyramids of Giza

The three Great Pyramids of Giza in Egypt are square pyramids. The largest and oldest was built more than 4,500 years ago as a tomb for the pharaoh Khufu. It was the world's tallest building for nearly 4,000 years. The pyramid is made of more than 2 million stone blocks weighing on average 2.5 tonnes. The pyramids are carefully positioned so that their four corners face North, South, East and West.

Flattening solids

If you unfold a solid into a flat shape, you produce a net. There may be several different ways to make a net from one kind of solid.

Net of a cube

The simplest way to unfold a cube is probably net number 4, but a cube can also be unfolded into 10 other nets.

All 11 of these nets can make a cube with a lid that opens like a Jack-in-the-box.

1
2
3
4
5
6
7
8
9
10
11

Can you see how each net can be folded into a cube?

Finding surface areas

Making nets is a great way of calculating the surface area of a solid. Here is the net of a square pyramid with **a base 1 cm across** and **sides that are triangles with a height of 1 cm**.

The square has an area of **1 cm²**. Remembering that the formula for the area of a triangle is

$$b \times \tfrac{1}{2}h$$

the area of each triangle is ½ cm². There are four triangles to add to the square, so the overall surface area of the pyramid is **3 cm²**.

1 cm

1

Here are two ideas of nets for you to make. (Remember to include the tabs on the side that you can fold over to stick the shape together.)

5 cm

5 cm

5 cm

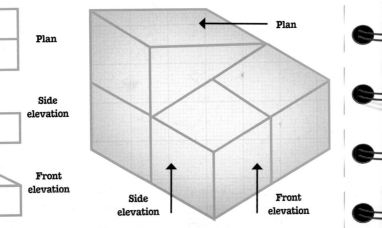

Plans and elevations

Architects make three-dimensional models and two-dimensional drawings of buildings to show their shape. Drawings made from overhead are called plans, while views from the front and sides are called elevations.

two-dimensional

Plan

Side elevation

Front elevation

three-dimensional

Plan

Side elevation

Front elevation

Spheres

A sphere is a solid on which all points on the surface are the same distance from the centre. A sphere is perfectly symmetrical and has no edges or corners.

Volume and surface area

We need the special number pi (see p.14) to work out a sphere's surface area and volume. These are the equations:

Surface area =
$$4\pi r^2$$

Volume =
$$^4/_3\pi r^3$$

radius (r)

Spheres in nature

A sphere has a special quality in that it is the shape with the maximum volume for the minimum surface area. For this reason, spheres appear in lots of places in nature where forces squeeze matter together, from stars and planets to raindrops.

Raindrops

High in the sky, raindrops form as tiny spheres of water. As they fall to the ground, the spheres become squashed at the bottom as the air pressure is greater at the bottom than at the top. If the drops become too big, they break apart to form smaller spheres.

The Sun and Earth

The most perfect natural sphere around us is the Sun. The Sun has a radius of

700,000 kilometres

It has a tiny bulge at the equator, meaning that it is 10 kilometres wider at its equator than from pole to pole. If scaled down to the size of a beachball, that difference would be less than the width of a human hair.

Equator

Like the Sun, Earth is also slightly squashed at the equator. This squashed shape is called an oblate spheroid.

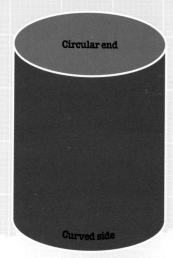

Circular end

Curved side

Cylinders, cones and toruses

Cylinders

A cylinder is a solid with flat, circular ends connected by one curved side. Like a prism (page 18), the cross-section of a cylinder is the same wherever you cut it.

A cake is the shape of a cylinder. To work out the **volume** of a cake (assuming it has the same thickness all the way through), you multiply the area of the circular base by its height, or thickness. So the **volume =**

$$\pi \times r^2 \times h$$

The **surface area** of a cylinder is the circumference of the circle × its height, plus the areas of the circular top and bottom. **Surface area =**

$$2\pi rh + 2\pi r^2$$

radius (r)

height (h)

Drinks cans are shaped as cylinders as this makes the packaging more efficient. A circle is the shape with the maximum area for its circumference, so more drink can be held in a cylindrical can than one shaped like a prism. The most efficient packaging would be a sphere, but spherical cans would roll off the shelves!

Cones

A cone is a solid with a **circular base** and one curved side ending in a point called its apex.

You can make a cone by rotating a right-angled triangle (in red) around its right angle.

Side length

Height

Radius

$\pi r^2 h$

$1/3 \pi r^2 h$

The formula for the volume of a cone is similar to that of a cylinder. So the volume =

$$\frac{1}{3} \pi \times r^2 \times h$$

where h is the cone's height. This means that the volume of a cone that fits tightly inside a cylinder is exactly one-third of the volume of the cylinder.

Mount Fuji in Japan is a volcano. Its cone-shaped slopes have been formed from molten lava flowing out in all directions during eruptions.

Torus

A torus is a ring-shaped solid. It is made by rotating a circle around a circular axis.

A torus made with a large circle looks like a doughnut. With a smaller circle, it looks more like a bicycle tyre.

axis

Size matters

The properties of a solid object change not just with its shape, but also with its size. For this reason, large animals need to be a different shape from smaller animals.

Why are polar bears so big?

A problem faced by all animals that live in the icy polar regions is how to keep warm. A polar bear has thick fur, but its huge size also helps it to conserve heat. To stay warm, you want to have as small a surface area relative to your mass as possible, as you lose heat through your skin. To see how a polar bear's huge size helps it keep warm, look at what happens when you scale up a sphere.

Using the formulas on page 22, the smaller sphere (**a**) has a volume of $4/3\pi$

It has a surface area of 4π

This means that its **surface area** is **three times greater than its volume**.

b

5 cm radius

a

1 cm radius

The larger sphere (**b**) has a volume of
$$500/3\pi$$
and a surface area of
$$100\pi$$

Its **volume** is **1.6 times greater than its surface area**. Volume increases by a cube of the scaling factor, but surface area only increases by a square of the scaling factor. If you want to keep warm in the Arctic, it pays to be big!

"So that's why I'm big boned"

Why do elephants have such thick legs?

An elephant has much thicker legs than a spider, relative to the rest of its body. A leg's strength depends on the area of its cross-section. As you scale up, the cross-section only increases by a square of the scaling factor, but the animal's weight increases by a cube. An elephant with spindly legs like those of a spider would buckle under its own weight.

Why King Kong would be weak at the knees

In the movie *King Kong*, Kong is a huge gorilla-shaped animal who stands nearly **8 metres tall**. Real-life gorillas are never more than 2 metres tall, so Kong is four times taller than a gorilla, but with the same relative dimensions to his body, head and legs.

A large gorilla weighs about **200 kg** and its leg bones have a cross-section area of about **10 cm²**. Standing on two legs, that means **200 kg** supported by **20 cm²**, which makes **10 kg per cm²**.

King Kong would weigh **200kg × 4³**, which is **12,800 kg**. His leg bones would have a cross-section area of **10 × 16 cm²**, which is **160 cm²**. Standing on two legs, **12,800 kg** would be supported by **320 cm²**, which makes **40 kg per cm²**, four times as much. Kong would have struggled to stand up, let alone climb the Empire State Building!

Quiz

1 How do you fit one hexagon together with three equilateral triangles to make **one equilateral triangle?**

2 Use **Pythagoras's theorem** to work out whether this staircase is a **right-angled triangle.**

3 Use **Pythagoras's theorem** to work out the **value of c.**

5

C

12

4 Face A has been **resized** to make face B. What was the **scale factor** used?

A

B

25   7

24

5 Look at the following **tessellations** of hexagons and triangles. Which pattern is **not semi-regular?**

a)

b)

c)

20cm

7 This wheel has a **diameter** of 20 cm. What is the **area** of the wheel?

8 Which three **Platonic solids** can be made using **triangles?**

9 What **shape** would you use to make a fair die with the **numbers 1 to 12** written on its faces?

6 You have one pizza that you want to share equally between **eight people**. If you slice the pizza into eight pieces, what will be the angle **between each radius?**

?°

10 What is the **volume** of this **prism**?

3 cm

5 cm

4 cm

Length 10 cm

11 This is a **hexagonal** pyramid.

a) How many **triangular faces** does it have?
b) How many **edges** does it have?

12 Which of the following is a **net of a cube?**

a)

b)

c)

13 What **solid** does this net **fold into**?

14 This cake has a **diameter** of 10 cm and a thickness of 2 cm. Use a calculator and the value of 3.14 for π to work out its **volume**.

diameter

height

30

Glossary

Acute angle
An angle that is less than 90°.

Cross-section
A shape that is made by cutting through a solid.

Equator
An imaginary line around Earth. The equator forms a circle that is the same distance from the North and South poles. It is 40,075 km long.

Geometry
The branch of mathematics that deals with points, lines, shapes, solids and dimensions.

Hypotenuse
The side of a right-angled triangle that is opposite the right angle. The hypotenuse is always the longest side of a right-angled triangle.

Obtuse angle
An angle that is more than 90°, but less than 180°.

Pi (π)
The number produced by dividing the circumference of a circle by its diameter. Pi equals about 3.14, but it is impossible to write it down exactly.

Platonic solids
The five regular solids. They have faces made of regular polygons, and the same number of faces meet at each vertex, or corner.

Polygon
A two-dimensional shape made with straight lines.

Polyhedron
A three-dimensional solid made by joining together polygons.

Right angle
An angle equal to 90°. A right angle is exactly one-quarter of a full turn.

Scale factor
The ratio of the length of an object in a drawing or model to the length of the real thing. With a scale factor of 1:100, 1 centimetre in a drawing would represent 1 metre in real life.

Symmetry
A property of a shape where it can be reflected or turned to make the same shape.

Tessellation
An arrangement of shapes to cover a surface without leaving gaps or overlapping. Also called tiling.

Transformation
A way of changing a shape using mathematical rules. A transformation may move the shape from one place to another, change its size or alter its shape by stretching or squashing it.

Translation
A transformation that moves a shape from one place to another.

Index

Answers

1.

2. $7^2 + 24^2 = 49 + 576 = 625$
    $= 25^2$. So it is a right-angled
    triangle.

3. $c^2 = 5^2 + 12^2 = 25 + 144$
    $= 169$. So $c = 13$

4. Scale factor ½

5. c is not semi-regular. The vertices are
    not all the same.

6. $360° ÷ 8 = 45°$

7. Area $= π × 10^2 = 3.14 × 100 = 314$ cm^2

8. Tetrahedron, octahedron, icosahedron.

9. A dodecahedron

10. The area of the base is 6 cm^2. Volume is
    6 cm^2 × 10 cm = 60 cm^3

11. a) 6 b) 12

12. c is a net of a cube

13. It is a square prism

14. $π × 5^2 × 2 = 50π = 157$ cm^3